The Night Walk

Story by Rose Inserra
Illustrations by Pat Reynolds

Alice lived in a small apartment
near the city.
Her parents had one bedroom,
and Alice shared the second bedroom
with her grandmother.
Alice's brother slept on the sofa bed
in the living room.

One week before her birthday,
Alice asked her mom
if she could have a sleepover.

"I'm sorry, Alice," her mom said.
"Our place is too small for a sleepover.
We don't have enough room."

"Why don't you have a picnic party
at the park?" said Mom.

"The park's **boring**," said Alice.
"Everyone in my class has sleepover parties."

"How about bowling?"
her brother suggested.

"It would cost too much
for everyone to go bowling," said Dad.
"We can't afford that."

Alice was very disappointed.
She wanted to invite her best friends
to her party.
They had all invited her to **their** parties.

"So when is your sleepover party, Alice?"
her friends kept asking.

"Next week," said Alice.
She just couldn't tell them
that she wasn't allowed to have a sleepover party.

That night, Alice couldn't sleep.
She started to cry.
Her grandma woke up and heard her.
"What's the matter, Alice?" she asked.

"I really wish I could have
a sleepover party," she sobbed.
"I've told all my friends
that I'm having a sleepover party."

"Don't cry, Alice," said Grandma.
"We'll think of something."

The next day, Grandma saw
a special advertisement in the newspaper.
It said:

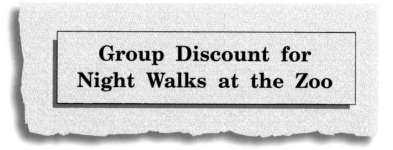

**Group Discount for
Night Walks at the Zoo**

Grandma called the zoo.
Then she called the parents
of Alice's best friends.
"We are having a birthday party for Alice
at the zoo next Friday," Grandma told them.
"Please meet us at the entrance to the zoo
at 7:30 in the evening."

The parents were surprised.
It would be quite dark by 7:30.

"It's a Night Walk party," explained Grandma.
"A zookeeper takes visitors for a walk
around the zoo in the dark.
The children will be able to see
the nocturnal animals
that sleep during the day."

The parents made a list of things
that Grandma asked them to bring.
They promised to keep the party a secret.

Then Mom and Grandma told Alice
she was going to have
a special kind of party after all.
"Please, Mom," Alice begged.
"Tell me what kind of party I'm having."

"It's Grandma's secret.
It's her birthday present to you," said Mom.

"But we'll give you a clue," said Grandma.
"You'll need a jacket."

"And a flashlight," said Mom.

"Why do I need a flashlight?" asked Alice.

"You'll see," said Grandma.

On Friday evening, Alice and her family
packed the car with the picnic things.
Then they set off to meet Alice's friends.

They stopped in the zoo parking lot.
"The zoo! At night?" said Alice.
"No one goes to the zoo at night!"
Then she saw all her friends
waiting by the entrance with their parents.

The zookeeper came out to meet them.
He counted them as he led them inside.
"Everyone stay together," he said.
"We don't want to lose anyone!"
It was very exciting.

Everything about the zoo
seemed bigger and scarier at night.
At first, Alice and her friends
couldn't see much, but slowly
things started to appear in the moonlight.
They saw moving shapes and glowing eyes.
"Those are the foxes," said the keeper.

An owl hooted and swooped near by.

An opossum
scurried up
a tree trunk.

They saw a raccoon hunting for mice,

and a skunk waddling along.

A kiwi rushed
out of the ferns
and then rushed
back again.

Strange calls and hoots
seemed to come from everywhere.
The zoo at night was a very **noisy** place.

When the Night Walk was finished,
Dad lifted the big picnic basket
from the car, and spread out a blanket.
They all sat down to drink hot chocolate
and to eat popcorn.
Then Alice cut her cake.

"This is better than any sleepover party,"
said one of her friends.

Alice looked at Grandma and smiled.
"Thank you," she said.   "That was **fun**!"